Guitar World P[...]
The Bonehead's Guide to Amps

Published by Hal Leonard Corporation
in cooperation with Harris Publications, Inc.
and Guitar World Magazine
Guitar World is a registered trademark
of Harris Publications, Inc.

HAL•LEONARD® CORPORATION

7777 W. BLUEMOUND RD. P.O. BOX 13819 MILWAUKEE, WI 53213

Guitar World Presents

The Bonehead's Guide to Amps

by Dominic Hilton

◆ Executive Producer
Brad Tolinski

◆ Producer
Carol Flannery

◆ Book Packager, Designer
Ed Uribe for Dancing Planet MediaWorks™

◆ Cover and Inside Illustrations
Jim Ryan

Foreword

While collecting some images for this book, I came across an old photo of my first amp. This three-watt beast was about the size of a cereal packet, had built-in tremolo, and had come from Woolworth's department store, a place not particularly renowned for killer amp tones. As I'd blown all my savings on a decrepit used Stratocaster and the obligatory overdrive pedal, this was all I could afford. I figured it was just an amp, and amps just made stuff louder, right? The sad, fizzy squeals it produced, however, were far from inspiring, and even further from the sounds on my AC/DC albums. Even with the help of a graphic EQ "borrowed" from the family stereo and a friend's booster pedal, it just got a little louder, a lot nastier, and was starting to make my fillings ache.

The epiphany occurred when I got to plug into my friend's new Marshall stack. As 100 watts of ineptly played Iron Maiden riffs crunched out of my guitar, I realized that amps don't just make squealy stuff louder, they make it sound awesome! After my Woolworth's warrior bought the farm with a final loud quack, I knew what had to be done. Many months and paper routes later, I bought a small Marshall combo that did a great impression of AC/DC and didn't make my teeth hurt. If you think, like I did, that amps are the boring side of guitar playing, then I hope this book helps change your mind and steers you clear of any Woolworth's squealers still lurking out there.

~DH

═══════════════════ ≈ ═══════════════════

The author would like to thank Brad Tolinski and Paul Riario at Guitar World magazine, Jim Ryan for his superb cartoons, Ed Uribe at Dancing Planet MediaWorks, Neville Marten and Sarah Clark at Guitarist magazine, Bean, and all those unruly amp manufacturers for the photos.

═══════════════════ ≈ ═══════════════════

About the Author:

DOMINIC HILTON is a freelance writer and incurable gearhead who enjoys spreading the word for Guitar World, Guitar World Acoustic, Guitarist, Bassist and Total Guitar magazines. He won't rest until he finds the lost tone of Atlantis.

Table of Contents

Introduction   **7**

Construction   **9**

    Combo   11

    Stack   12

    Rack   13

How They Work   **15**

    The Cabinet   16

    The Speaker   19

    The Preamp   22

    Tone Controls   24

    Power Amp   25

    Channels   27

    Boost   28

    Reverb   28

    Vibrato   29

    Chorus   30

    Effects Loop   31

    Other Switches and Sockets   32

Different Types   **35**

    Tube Versus Solid-State   36

    Hybrid Amps   39

Digital Amps   39

Vintage Versus Modern   41

Examples in Close-Up   43

Buyer's Guide   55

Application: Power   56

Application: Features   61

Budget   62

Used Gear   64

Testing, Testing...   65

The Essential Checklist   66

Maintenance   69

Safety   70

Cleaning, Transportation and Storage 71

Tube Replacement   72

Getting Your Tone   73

Setting Your Sounds   74

Multi-Channels   75

Using Effects   76

Introduction ^{1.}

When someone is struck by the urge to join the thousands, maybe even millions, of electric guitar players throughout the world, strange things happen. Brochures are hoarded and memorized and magazine articles are scoured for details. A zombie-like state occurs outside music store windows, where fanatical debates are waged with strange words like *humbucker* and *wah-wah*. Unfortunately, most of this energy is usually directed at the guitar itself, with the amplifier, the other half of this potent team, receiving just a few hasty decisions. This is a terrible mistake, because the amplifier is an exciting and inspiring tool, and, when used properly, can be an instrument all its own. The aim of this book is to explain how these boisterous boxes work, so that you can get a clear idea of which models would suit you best and learn to get the most from yours. With a little knowledge, your amp can become an ally, instead of ending up as nothing more than an ugly coffee table.

Since musical amplifiers first appeared back in the 1920s, they have changed considerably in some aspects—they've gotten bigger and louder—but hardly at all in others. They're fundamentally made with the same technology. In fact, the first music hall amplifier systems used less power than a single modern practice amp, and people had to whisper when the band was on! Rock 'n' roll quickly put a stop to that, but many of the classic guitar amps we'll be looking at were conceived all those decades ago. Today, we guitarists are spoiled with choice, from delightful collector's pieces to sonic weapons of mass destruction. Welcome to eccentric and harmonious Ampsville!

2. Construction

Just Add Water!

Amplifier systems are basically composed of four parts: a **preamp**, a **tone control system**, a **power amp** and the **speaker system**. The signal from the guitar's **pickup** enters the amplifier through the **input** and is boosted by the preamp. The preamp is used to beef up the relatively weak guitar signal after its journey down the long cable and provides a stronger signal for the amp's circuitry to work with. The boosted signal is then shaped by the tone control system. This system may be a single control or a more complex series of controls, which determine how the guitar will sound when heard through the speakers.

The power amp is the device that provides the necessary volume. It does this by taking the signal from the preamp and tone sections and boosting it many times over. This process is illustrated in the following simple diagram:

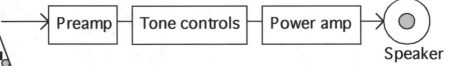

This whole system basically "translates" the notes being played on the guitar into its own electrical language. This electrical signal can then be shaped, increased, and pumped through the speakers—which turn it back into vibrations we recognize as sound.

Most amplifiers can produce a range of different sounds, or **tones**, by adjusting the various controls. However, different amps also have quite different and very distinct characteristics in terms of their overall sound and the way in which they respond to the guitar. For this reason, certain amps are favored for particular styles of music.

Another major consideration when choosing an amplifier is the power rating, or **output**. This is measured in **watts** and determines how loud the amplifier is capable of being played. Live performances normally require an amp with a high output of 50 to 100 watts, whereas practicing and recording can be done with an amp of 10 to 30 watts, or even less. The output wattage is governed by the size of the power amp.

Before we take a closer look at the inner workings of these parts, let's introduce ourselves to the three most common amplifier systems we will come across.

Combo

These are so called because they are a combination of all of the amplifier components in one unit. The **cabinet** holds all of the necessary circuitry, along with one to four speakers. This is the most portable  of the three systems we will discuss.

These popular amps range in size from tiny practice units to large and powerful models suitable for live playing on any size stage or venue.

Famous combo users and abusers include Brian May, Paul Weller, Stevie Ray Vaughan and Buddy Guy.

Stack

This impressive format houses the amplifier circuitry separately from the speakers, in the amp **head**. The head is then "stacked" on top of the speaker **cabinets** (or **cabs**)—hence

the name. This system allows various combinations of speakers to be used—up to a total of eight. It also offers further control of the sound. The powerful nature of these amps means they are most often used for live playing.

Famous stack users and abusers include Jimi Hendrix, Angus Young, Eddie Van Halen and Randy Rhoads.

Rack

This is the most complex system of the three under discussion (the combo, stack and rack). It combines separate components that are placed into a **rack**—hence the term "rack system." This allows the player to build an amplifier

system from a large range of different components and generally includes various **effects units** as well. There is no limit to what can be included in a rack, but the most basic configuration will have a combined preamp and tone control unit, with a separate power amp unit driving the speaker cabinets. Also included will be a number of units for special effects such as distortion, chorus, flange, reverb and any number of other aural enhancements. These units all combine to provide the player with a truly powerful and versatile setup.

These systems offer players virtually unlimited control over their sound for both live performance and recording work, and are truly the systems of choice for those players seeking the varied scenarios that they can accommodate. It should be noted, though, that all of this power and versatility comes at a price, as rack systems can be expensive and complicated to configure and use.

Famous rack users and abusers include Dave Gilmour, Steve Vai, Adrian Belew and Steve Lukather.

How They Work

In this chapter we will examine how amps work, along with a look at their different parts and components. We'll also check out some of the additional features that appear on the many different models.

The Cabinet

The cabinet is the protector of your amp's delicate parts. Whether used to house speakers, heads or combos, its primary function is to keep sharp objects, sticky liquids, audience members and other harmful things away from the fragile innards of the amplifier. Cabinets are all made from some type of wood. High-grade plywood is the most common material, and medium density fiberboard (MDF) is found in the cheaper models. Fancy hardwood cabinets appear in some of the expensive or custom amplifiers.

Combo with snakeskin-covered cabs

The wood is shaped and joined before being covered with some kind of protective coating. Traditionally this is a textured vinyl material called Tolex, which is tough and waterproof, and commonly black or cream in color. Modern variations include coverings made from tear-resistant synthetic fibers that are either glued on in sheets, like Tolex, or sprayed directly onto the wood. Some companies have caught on to the guitar player's love of eye-catching finishes, and offer amps in bright-colored, animal-print, pearlescent, leather or even polished-metal coverings. These may not alter the sound of the amp, but if you want a combo that looks like a cow, it's now a possibility.

The amp circuitry is fitted to a metal **chassis** that is bolted inside the cabinet, usually so that the knobs and switches are recessed out of harm's way. Speakers are installed through a hole on a front-facing board called the **baffle**. The baffle is normally hidden behind the **grille cloth** which is a mesh or fabric that is sonically transparent; in other words, it doesn't muffle or alter the sound. Some cabinets have metal "kick-proof" grilles, which may be an option to

consider if you intend to tour around rowdy venues. The other cabinet hardware you can expect are **carrying handles**, plastic or metal **corner protectors**, and, on larger equipment, **casters**. These save on backache by allowing gear to be wheeled into position.

Speaker cabinet with casters and side handles

Combo with open-backed design

It is important to realize that the actual structure of the cabinet can have a considerable effect on the sound of an amp. The most noticeable sonic difference will be between **open-backed** and **closed-back** designs. Cabinets with a partially enclosed rear panel, or open back, are common on combos and allow the sound from the speaker to disperse from the front and rear of the amp. This produces a more "airy" and ambient tone than that of cabinets with a fully sealed, or closed-back, design. Closed-back cabinets force the sound through the front of the speaker, which projects and enhances the low frequencies of the sound, adding focus and "thump." To a lesser degree, the resonant properties of the cabinet materials can accent or mute certain frequencies, accounting for the differences in tone between similar designs.

18

Closed-back cab

The Speaker

In the same way that the guitar pickup uses a coil and magnet to change sound vibrations into electricity, so does the speaker use the same components to reverse the process.

19

When the electrical signal arrives at the speaker from the amp, it moves through a cylindrical coil inside a doughnut-shaped magnet. This forces the coil to vibrate within the magnetic field, which is exaggerated by the thin paper speaker cone. This effect can be compared to blowing through a tissue-covered comb. This slaps the surrounding air molecules into action, enabling us to hear—and, at high volumes, feel—the sound.

The magnet, coil and cone are all held in place by a metal frame, and many of these designs have remained unchanged for decades. As you will see, this is just one of the many quirks of guitar amps that rely mainly on old technology to produce pleasing tones. For this reason many of the speakers used in modern amps are based on vintage designs such as those originally made by Celestion, Fane and Vox. The speakers used in modern audio equipment, like stereos, are powerful and efficient, with a high tolerance for **distortion**, enabling them to clearly reproduce the sound from a CD, microphone or practically any audio source. Guitar speakers have different properties and are less efficient. When driven hard by the amplifier they start to distort, adding a pleasing warmth and edge to the sound. Although most amplifiers and speakers are designed to minimize distortion, it is an essential ingredient for guitar amps. The powerful, thick, fuzzy or crunchy tone is synonymous with the electric guitar, and some of that sound is produced by the speaker. In the era before guitar amps with built-in distortion, players would actually slash their speaker cones with razors to enhance this effect. This is no longer necessary, and certainly not recommended. Certain styles of music like jazz and country demand a clean tone, meaning a tone without any distortion. In this case more efficient speaker designs that produce a clear sound are favored, such as models produced by companies like ElectroVoice and Eminence.

4x12 cab

2x12 cab

Speakers are described in terms of their diameter in inches. The most common size is 12", although 10" and 15" speakers are sometimes used. Small practice amps use speakers between 4" and 8". The speaker format description is abbreviated by combining the number of speakers, their size and their cabinet type. For example a **2x12 combo** describes a combo amp with two 12" speakers, and a **4x10 cab** refers to a separate cabinet containing four 10" speakers. Cabs may also be described as **slope** or **straight-front**, to differentiate between cabs that have the grille partially angled backward and those with a flat grille. Each projects the sound in different directions. The other most common formats are 1x12 combo, 4x10 combo, 1x12 cab, 2x12 cab and 4x12 cab.

The Preamp

In the world of guitars, the term "preamp" can refer to a number of things: the circuitry in electro-acoustic or active guitars, a stand-alone effects pedal or, in the case of a rack

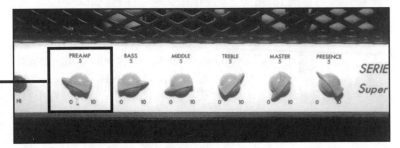

system, the entire tone-shaping unit that is separated from the power amp. However, in this section we will look at the preamp that is part of the amplifier itself, which is also responsible for producing distortion. If you still haven't grasped what distortion is about, just pick out any blues, rock or metal CD from your collection and listen to the guitars. From the singing sting of B. B. King to the roar of the Who to the almighty crunch of AC/DC to the aggressive grind of Metallica, you're always hearing some degree of amp distortion.

Back in the 1960s, the only way to get distortion from an amp was to turn it up—way up. In doing so the amplifier circuitry and speakers would start to overload to produce that sought-after **overdrive** sound. This was obviously a problem if you wanted distortion at a level that wouldn't get you in trouble with your neighbors. The solution arrived in the '70s with the invention of **master volume** amps.

By including a small amplifier before the main amp, or power amp, it was possible to push the first stage of the circuit into overdrive while governing the overall volume with a master volume control on the power amp. This small amplifier is the preamp, and it has its own volume control, generally called the **gain** control. As the gain control is turned up, so the level of distortion increases. With the control only slightly on, the amp will produce its cleanest sound. When the gain is fully up, the sound will be at maximum distortion. The settings in between these limits will yield various degrees of crunch and softly overdriven tones, depending on the characteristics of the amplifier.

If an amp is described as being **high-gain**, it means that the gain can deliver a high level of distortion, beyond the more restrained tones of vintage-type amps. Some amp models have several gain controls, often referred to as **pre-** and **post-**gain, which allow different types of distortions to be produced from the interaction of the two controls.

If an amp has low gain, or none at all, then distortion can be added using one of the many distortion pedals available. These offer a huge range of different distortion tones, and

many are affordably priced, from around $50 on up. Boss, DOD, Ibanez, Tech 21 and Pro Co are companies offering some of the most popular units.

Tone Controls

In its simplest form the tone control is a single knob that governs the overall balance of the low and high **frequencies** of the amp's sound. If the control is turned down, the sound

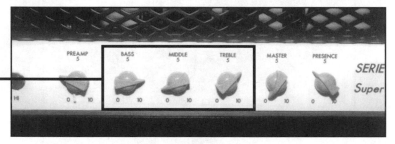

will be muted with the low frequencies, or **bass**, dominating. Fully up, the sound will be bright and sharp as the high frequencies, or **treble**, are exaggerated. It is more common for an amp to have two or more tone controls that govern the amount of a particular area of frequencies. If the amp has two controls, they will be bass and treble; three will be bass, **mid** and treble; and four will be bass, **lower- mid**, **upper-mid** and treble. The more tone controls an amp has, the more control the player has over his or her sound. By adjusting the various levels of the different tone controls in conjunction with the gain control, many different sounds can be pulled from the same amp.

All of the controls on a guitar amp are marked with a scale, most commonly 0 to 10. When trying an amp, or looking for sounds, it is best to start with the tone controls set **flat**, meaning that all are turned to setting 5. This produces  a sound with all the frequencies at the same level and best demonstrates the natural sound of the amp. The various controls can then be used to add or subtract certain frequencies to find the desired tone. We will look at some basic tone settings later in this book.

Power Amp

This section of the amplifier system does all the hard work, delivering the shaped signal from the preamp and tone controls to the speakers, with a hefty shove in volume. In

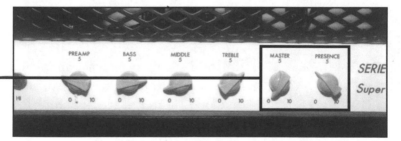

many cases the power amp will have only a single master volume control to govern the output volume. Some amplifiers do have additional controls in this section—a common feature is a **presence** control—which is like a master tone control. This is particularly useful when you have set up a

25

sound you like, but, after you use another guitar or move the amp to a different place, the sound seems to have drifted and become dull or overly bright. The presence control can tune the overall tone to compensate for these changes.

Like the preamp, the power amp also starts to produce its own distortion when driven at higher volumes. This adds another desirable ingredient to the complex structure of the amp's tone. Obviously this requires the amp to be working near its maximum output, which can be problematic. Some amps feature a **power mode** switch that enables the wattage of the power amp to be halved, so that it can be pushed harder at a lower volume. Another option is a product like Marshall's Powerbrake, which is a heavy-duty volume control capable of absorbing the power of a flat-out amp to deliver the same tone at a lower volume. Not exactly an efficient use of electricity, but worth the extra bills for harnessing the sound of an amp on meltdown.

This Peavey 5150 Combo features a focus and resonance control.

Modern amplifiers may also include a **focus** or **resonance** control. This alters the way in which the power amp and speakers interact and can be adjusted to produce a loose, airy tone or a tighter, more punchy response. With these controls the sound of both closed- and open-backed cabinets can be emulated from one format.

Another device that is sometimes mentioned in connection with the power amp section is the **rectifier**. Although all amps use one of these to process the incoming AC electricity, it was found that, like many amp components, it has a bearing on the actual tone. For this reason companies may offer different types of rectifiers (e.g. **triode** or **pentode**) and even several versions in the same amp, allowing the player to switch between them for different sounds.

Channels

Like TVs, lots of amps have **channels** too. Many amplifiers have two channels, although some are available with three

or even four. Essentially they allow several different tones to be set up, and the player can switch between them as required. The simplest version of this is to have two gain controls, which can be preset with different amounts of distortion and selected via a **foot switch**. As both channels still use the same tone controls, there is usually a compromise in overall sound, as the optimum tone settings for clean sounds are often quite different from those used for distortion. However, many modern amps, including some less expensive models, feature **independent** channels. In addition to having individual gain controls, they also include separate tone controls, allowing several completely different sounds to be preset. This format usually includes separate volume controls for each channel for complete flexibility. In most cases these channels are voiced to be suitable for different ranges of sounds, such as one channel for clean sounds, the other for distortion.

Boost

A simple control that allows the player to set a fixed amount of boost to the sound that can be activated by a foot switch. This enables the volume to be temporarily increased when needed, e.g., to drown out the keyboard player during the guitar solos.

Reverb

An increasing number of modern amps feature built-in multiple effects, but traditionally only a handful of basic

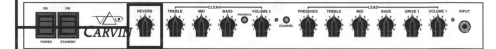

effects are commonplace inside amplifiers. **Reverb** is one such effect and a popular ingredient in many models that

adds dramatic texture to the tone. This device normally uses a number of springs in the circuitry, hence the term **spring reverb**. These springs are contained in a box-shaped **tray**, or **tank**, bolted to the inside of the cabinet. Reverb produces an effect akin to playing in a large room by adding extra depth and reverberation to the sound. The simplest way to describe this sound is *big*; it's like adding an extra dimension to the notes played.

As the reverb control is increased the effect becomes more pronounced, with one note continuing to sound as the next is played, almost like an echo. At the highest setting your guitar can sound as if it is being played from miles down a deep ravine—pretty impressive for a few simple springs. This effect is loved by many guitarists and is often used for soulful leads or to "loosen up" a rhythm sound.

If you accidentally bump a reverb-equipped amp you will hear an almighty rumbling sound. Don't worry, this is just the reverb springs moving a bit more than they should. It may sound cool, but don't make a habit of it!

Vibrato

Also known as **tremolo** (although not actually the same effect), it is often misnamed, or the two effects are combined to mean the same thing. This is another traditional amp effect beloved by players with a taste for "retro" sounds.

Although not nearly as common as reverb, vibrato does appear on a number of vintage and modern amps. This effect causes the sound to pulse from a fast warbling shimmer to a slow pronounced stutter, with all gradations in between. As such, the effect can be used to add subtle movement or dramatic on-off bursts of sound. Check out R.E.M.'s *Monster* album for a classic use of this effect.

Vibrato is adjusted with two controls: **speed** (or **rate**) and **depth** (or **intensity**). The speed can be increased from a slow pulse to the maximum speed, where the effect is inaudible. This

is the "off" setting on some amps. This speed can be matched to the tempo of a song so that the guitar pulses in time with the other instruments, lending an interesting effect. The depth controls the amplitude of the pulse, and ranges from a slight quiver to an exaggerated beat of sound.

Amplifiers renowned for their vibrato effect include the very collectable Fender Vibrolux and the modern Mesa Engineering Trem-O-Verb.

Chorus

This effect didn't appear on amps until the 1970s, most noticeably with Roland's Jazz Chorus combos, renowned for

their ultra-clean and rich, shimmering tones. A chorus essentially does what most bands practice hard to avoid: it makes two guitar parts sound out of tune and out of time with each other. The chorus does this by taking the amp's guitar signal and doubling it with another that has been slightly detuned and, in a similar way to vibrato, pulses at a given rate. The result is a thick, lush sound that has been "humanized" to sound like several guitars playing at once. At the height of its range the effect takes on the characteristics of vibrato, lending the guitar the gutsy warble of the Hammond organ, the classic keyboard sound of any '70s supergroup.

As it appears on the amp, chorus has two controls: **rate** and **depth**—confusingly similar to vibrato controls. Rate sets the speed of the sound undulations: slow and gentle to fast and shimmery. Depth determines the amount of detuning, or difference in pitch, between the effected and original signal, from subtle to warble. This effect is typically used with a clean tone and the controls set around their midpoints to produce a sweet but not overly effected sound. However, as with any effect, experimentation can yield some very interesting sounds.

Effects Loop

During the 1970s a multitude of new guitar effects appeared that heralded the end of the simple "fuzz box and

wah-wah into the amp" setup, which was the height of signal processing at the time. Instead of simply hooking up a couple of pedals, guitarists could now string together a whole spread of stompboxes in a frenzy of patch cords and curly leads. One problem our loon-panted forebears discovered with this stompbox smorgasbord was that not all effects sounded good plugged straight into the amp.

The cause of the problem was the distortion generated in the preamp section of the amplifier. Some effects work best before distortion, others work best acting on a signal that has already been distorted.

For example, a **delay** or **echo** pedal will sound fine plugged into a clean amp, but if the gain is turned up, it sounds like a mess. However, put the delay after the distortion, and it sounds brilliant.

To get around this problem, amp designers invented the **effects loop**, which allows effects to be separated into those that work best plugged straight in and those that need to be linked between the preamp and the power amp—that is, after the distortion.

The following diagram shows the effects loop position in the amp:

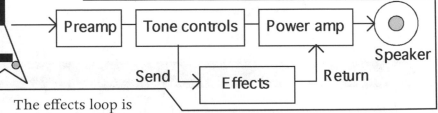

The effects loop is usually found on the rear panel of an amp and consists of two sockets marked **send** and **return**. By connecting a guitar lead from the send socket into the chosen effects, and another from the output of the effects into the return socket, the effects can be switched in and out of the gap between the preamp and power amp. The result? Slinky effected distortion instead of messy distorted effects. There may also be additional controls in this section to govern the signal traveling through the loop. Often this is a **blend** control that determines the level of the effected signal in the sound; you can blend in a small amount for a more subtle effect or mix in lots for more outrageous sounds. Occasionally there will be separate send and return **level** controls for more flexibility. We will look at some effects loop applications in the last chapter.

Other Switches and Sockets

Some amps bristle with switches, lights and knobs for all sorts of different modes and functions. For the sake of simplicity we will look at the most common features that may appear on your amp. One area that can be confusing is the input section. It may be a single jack socket, posing no problem, or it may include other features. Some amps have two inputs marked **hi** and **lo**, or one socket with an adjacent switch marked in the same way. This usually means that guitars with a high output should be plugged into the hi socket/setting, and vice versa. On some amps it can mean  the opposite. Either way, no need to worry, simply try your guitar in both sockets/settings and go with the one that sounds best—simple. Similarly, some amps have an extra **bright** socket or switch, which has a brighter sound than the normal input. Again, decide with your ears which one suits you best.

Many amps have a **speaker out** socket(s) and an **imped-ance** switch on the rear panel to accommodate different speaker formats. If you decide to change or use additional

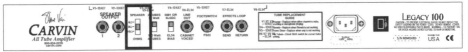

Impedance switch

speakers, then the switch needs to be adjusted to the correct value. The math involved is pretty confusing, so seek professional advice if the speakers you intend to use are not clearly marked with their impedance value (which is meas-ured in **ohms**).

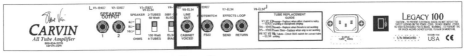

Recording output

An increasingly common feature is a **balanced recording output** on the rear panel of modern amps. This allows the tone of the amp to be recorded without using a microphone and playing at high volumes. Depending on the model, this output may include extra circuitry that more closely mimics the actual sound of the power amp and speaker sections. This renders a more realistic tone.

Fuse holder

Finally, there should be one or more **fuse holders** mounted on the rear of the chassis. These protect the user as well as the circuitry from overloads and short circuits. These should be left alone and intact if the amp is working correctly. More information on this subject is presented in the Safety section of Chapter 6.

If the amp you own or intend to buy has other features not mentioned here, chances are it will be an additional tone function of some kind. However, don't risk yourself or the amp. If you are unsure, consult the manual and/or your friendly salesperson.

Different Types

By now the various knobs, switches, sockets and functions of the amplifier should no longer be a mystery, but the phrases **tube** and **solid-state** probably are. Had this book been written 10 years ago, this hotly debated subject would have been covered in the opening pages. However, with the many recent developments in amp design it would be misleading to attach so much importance to this difference in circuitry, especially for the first-time buyer. So what are we talking about? Basically, the type of electronic components used to build an amp, and another of those old-technology quirks of amp design.

Tube Versus Solid-State

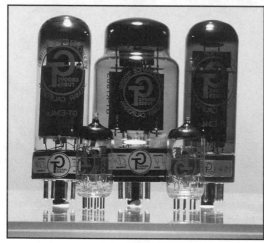

Tubes

The very first guitar amplifiers appeared in the early 1930s and used devices called tubes, the cutting edge of electronic technology at the time. These primitive—and very delicate—components are housed in glass and use a complex structure of filaments and conducting surfaces to process the electrical signal. This prewar technology remained at the heart of guitar amplification until the 1970s when it was hit by the silicon revolution and superseded by

Transistors

Tube amp

transistors. The solid-state amp was born. These new amp components were smaller, cheaper, more durable and more efficient, and amps changed accordingly. As the world enjoyed cheap miniaturized goodies like the transistor radio and pocket calculators, guitarists had cheaper, more reliable amps and a wealth of new effects. The big "but" came when guitarists realized that, for the greater part,

Solid-state amp

many of these new amps sounded cold and nasty. Many players and amp companies quickly drifted back to the old ways and the cumbersome technology of the glowing tube, leaving solid-state amps to limp on as the poor man's substitute for the real thing. This prejudice has remained among guitarists, even though the amp is possibly the only modern device that still uses tubes and manufacturers have to rely on obscure sources in China and Russia to build these electronic fossils.

There is no denying that tube amps sound good, which is why they still sell in the thousands. So why buy solid-state? Well, amp technology has come a long way since the '70s and clever circuitry exists that can do a fine impression of a tube amp at a fraction of the cost. Check out Peavey's

Digital-modeling amp

TransTube amp as an example. Furthermore, with the advent of **digital modeling**, a sort of computer simulation of classic amp tones, it has become very difficult to distinguish between real tube tone and integrated-circuit-powered mimics. Another big plus for solid-state is its durability. Tubes are fragile and, like lightbulbs, burn out with time. A replacement set can cost several hundred dollars for complex amps. Also, solid-state amps are more likely to work after taking a tumble. In conclusion, it would be a mistake to regard any of the excellent solid-state amps available today as a compromise. Some are actually preferred over tube amps for their tighter, grittier distortion. For example, Randall's solid-state stacks have been recently re-introduced due to the high demand by modern hard rock and metal players.

Hybrid Amps

One path many amp companies have taken to get over the tube/solid-state dilemma is the **hybrid** amp, using both technologies. By combining real tubes in the preamp with a solid-state power amp it is possible to produce a naturally warm and smooth tone. This effective compromise often appears on cheaper models, such as Marshall's popular Valvestate series, and only having one or two tubes to worry about makes maintenance cheaper.

Digital Amps

To complete the description of different amp circuits we also need to take a closer look at digital amplifiers. Digital technology first entered the guitar world in

Silicon chips

effects like the **digital delay**, where silicon chips were used to produce quieter and smoother effects. Since then companies like Roland,

Yamaha, Line 6, Johnson and Tech 21 have all harnessed the power of digital and "discrete" technology in various ways—for example, to generate the actual tone of the amp and emulate classic sounds with the digital modeling mentioned above. While these amps are still considered solid-state, their additional use of digital processing allows them to produce complex tones, often with a variety of on-board effects. One complaint made about digitally produced tone is its slightly cold and sterile sound—the same argument you hear about CDs versus vinyl recordings. For this reason some of these products contain non-digital, **analog circuits,** for added warmth. These analog sections may use transistors or even real tubes (like hybrid amps) in a bizarre combination of the ancient and the cutting edge, a common recipe in rack-mounted systems. Digital technology is certainly a powerful tool for guitarists but it still looks unlikely to put the much-loved, 70-year-old tube into retirement for some years yet.

Without wallowing too far into the technobabble of **MIDI** (Musical Instrument Digital Interfacing), it is certainly worth mentioning its existence. Digital guitar amps and processors speak the same language as computers, which means they can use computers to manipulate and enhance their capabilities. If you stumbled across the most amazing tone you ever heard from your amp, it used to mean taking out a notepad and carefully marking down all the settings, any effects and their settings, and just about everything but the wind direction. With the new generation of digital amps, you simply press a button marked "store" and that sound can be retrieved at any time, along with hundreds of others. If the amp has MIDI connections, these memories can be stored and combined or controlled by the computer, and other **MIDI-compatible** devices. This allows you to do all sorts of unnatural things with guitar tones using synthesizers, sequencers and powerful software. A boon for recording and general outlandishness, MIDI can, however, become far closer to computer programming than spontaneous jamming. Taken to an extreme, you can ditch your amp and effects, fit a **MIDI pickup** to any old plank of a guitar hooked up to a computer and still produce the tone of sought-after vintage setups. You could also replicate the sound of a pod of whales moshing in custard, and just about anything else. It may not be for the amplifier purist, but the possibilities are certainly boggling.

Vintage Versus Modern

 Like all areas of guitar-related equipment, the amp does not escape the vintage-modern debate. The deal is that some players prefer to stick with the old sound and looks of the earlier amps; others prefer the tone and/or complexity of their control-encrusted successors. If you find yourself hankering after the classic tones of elderly rock stars and deceased bluesmen, then vintage-type amps will probably be the choice. To be truly authentic, some players track down an original vintage piece, but as inspiring as these old-timers can be, they have their problems. First, many are hot collector's pieces and command top dollar; second, you

may not want to rely on an amp that is twice as old as you are. Thankfully amp companies have long since realized the value of their historical designs and created a generous spread of **reissues**, which are true to the originals but safer, cheaper and brand-spanking new. Marshall, Fender and Vox are some of the companies that regularly offer reissues. Alternately, there are many new amps designed to do the vintage thing. Peavey, Carvin, Matchless and Washburn all offer "new-vintage" models, some at very reasonable prices. These can usually be spotted dressed in **tweed** Tolex and **chickenhead** knobs, to underline their tonal intentions.

Players opting for modern amps are generally those thirsting for a double helping of gain, although the increased control options of multiple channels, added effects and even MIDI compatibility are other big factors. There is a huge range of modern amps to choose from: budget high-gain solid-state combos for riff-mongers (Peavey, Laney, Carlsbro, Crate), monster tube-driven function-laden combos and stacks (Mesa Engineering, Rivera, Soldano,

Marshall), and high-powered rack systems worthy of the USS *Enterprise*, with amps from the latter four companies along with complex processors by Rocktron, ADA, DigiTech and Yamaha, to name but a few.

Examples in Close-Up

Rather than attempt to cover every amp on the market, let's look at a selection of models that represent the most popular amplifier styles. Although we will be looking at a single model from each manufacturer, bear in mind that some companies produce a whole range of amps. Very few specialize in single formats or specific price ranges, and the same company could make everything from a $200 practice combo to a $3,000 stack, vintage and modern styles, tube and solid-state, etc.

Starting with the simplest and working up, it doesn't get any more simple than the **Pignose** combo. This company has been making these solid-state, leatherette-covered babies for over 25 years and every guitarist seems to own one at some time in their life. Packing just a few watts  through a fist-sized speaker, the Pignose is still capable of making some fine noise. The trademark "pig snout" is the only control, combining an on/off switch with a master volume. Turn it up and it gets louder and dirtier, reaching a buzzy peak of bluesy overdrive. Although described as a practice amp, this little piggy is beloved of buskers and

43

travelers for its on-board battery power. It is supremely portable and surprisingly sassy, and has become a real classic.

Just a little beefier is the renowned **Fender Champ** combo, which first appeared way back in 1947, blowing four watts of tube power through a single 6" speaker. Since then the design of the Champ has changed many times. Extra tone controls were added to the original single on/off/volume control, 8" speakers were substituted, some models gained reverb and even vibrato, and later models appeared as solid-state versions. Whichever incarnation of this single-channeled mite you may come across, it is typically enjoyed for its clean punch and unexpectedly hairy overdrive. It earned its place in musical history when Jimmy Page employed one, pushed to its limits, to record gargantuan guitar sounds on many Led Zeppelin records—quite an achievement for a student model practice amp.

The **Vox AC30** is another hallowed classic amp. This 2x12 combo was born in the UK in 1959 and was neither shy nor retiring when it came to distortion, especially with the legendary option of the "Top Boost" circuitry. Like other early amps it was offered with a spread of inputs, both high and low for each of its three shared channels—Normal, Brilliant and Vib/Trem—and housed one of the best vibrato circuits found in any amp. Rated at 30 watts, this tube-driven combo is loud enough to hold its own in most band

situations and has a very characteristic sound. The clean tones are warm and sinewy, but it is the singing wail of the AC30 overdrive that has earned it its reputation. For an example, pop on any Queen recording to hear Vox devotee Brian May coax his luscious trademark harmony leads from an excited AC30. The full pedigree originals fetch ridiculous prices, but superb reissues are now lovingly produced in a nostalgic corner of the U.K. Marshall factory.

The solid-state **Roland Jazz Chorus** combo is a historical odd ball that was saved from obscurity because, while its distortion sucked horribly, its sweet, chorused, clean sound was a triumph. The most desirable model is the **JC-120**, which combines two 60-watt power amps running in stereo through its two 12" speakers. The pioneering chorus circuitry added a dramatic dimension to the powerful, clean tone and was embraced by jazz and pop players, including the Police's Andy Summers. In a market where the phrase "'70s Japanese solid-state" is usually a design curse, the JC-120 continues to thrive in its original and reissued forms.

No amp roll call would be complete without the **Fender Twin Reverb**, the beefcake big brother of the Fender

combos. There are many Fender amps worthy of mention, but the Twin 2x12 combo is certainly one of the jewels in the Fender crown. Like most Fender products the Twin has appeared in many forms. The first models tickled their speakers with a modest 15 watts, but by 1979 they were frightening front-row ticket-holders with a Godzilla-like 135 watts. The Super Twin model added extra tubes for an even scarier 185 watts! These two-channel amps introduced many players to the glorious tone of spring reverb, and the high output certainly played a part in the development of the rock guitarist ego. Hot, fat and spanky cleans are just a few of the Twin's highlights; muscular crunch and punchy blues tones are also there for the taking, and some models feature vibrato as well as reverb. The characteristic distortion is not particularly high-gain but has a maverick attitude that allows it to sound psychotic and clear at the same time. The Twin is a highly collectable vintage amp, but the later models and current reissues continue to find favor amongst many modern players.

An unashamedly macho pinnacle of rock guitar amplification has to be the mighty **Marshall JCM 900** full stack. Although other companies produced head-and-cabinet amplifiers, often quaintly named **piggybacks**, it was the magnificent vision of a wall of quaking Marshall stacks that really put the hard in rock. The original Marshalls were actually attempts by the British company to copy the tone of Fender **Bassman** amps, but the use of different components and modified circuits led to one of the greatest amps in history.

Jim Marshall's company now produces a vast range of amplifiers, from solid-state practice amps to hybrids, stacks and rack-mounted units. It is, however, the stacks that really put Marshall on the map. Early models such as the **JTM 45** and **1959 100-Watt** heads were adopted by Jimi Hendrix, which catapulted them to stardom. Volume-beast Pete Townshend coaxed Marshall to further extremes, which resulted in two significant products. The first was the fabulous aggression of the 100-watt **Super Lead** head, featuring a pumped-up power amp to lay major tinnitus on Who fans. The second was a monstrous 8x12 cab, primarily designed to feed the showmanship excesses of the band. To allow for portability, this was split into two 4x12 cabs, and the full stack, as we now know it, became the familiar backdrop for many rock bands. Since then Marshall has introduced a succession of milestone amps: the '70s **Master Volume** series, the gnarly **JCM 800** and the modern, more complex multi-channel **Anniversary** and **JCM 2000** amps, capable of incendiary levels of gain as well as excellent clean sounds. Sitting comfortably in the middle is the **JCM 900**, with more gain than the JCM 800, but still retaining a simple two-channel-and-reverb recipe. This is one of the real, tough workhorses of the Marshall range and is very reliable for an all-tube amp. It excels in live performance, delivering a raunchy punch soaked in attitude and more output than most folks can handle. Anything above 7 on the master volume is inviting damage to your internal organs. The screaming lead tone and elephant-butt-kicking bass leave you in no doubt that you're plugged into a Marshall, modern, vintage or reissue.

The popularity of Fender, Marshall and Vox amps spawned a new breed of company, the builders of **superamps**. Most of

these companies have a background in modifying, or **hot-rodding**, classic amps to deliver more gain, extra functions or improved tone. Over time they used this knowledge to produce their own amplifiers. **Mesa Boogie** (arguably the pioneers of independent channels), **Rivera** and **Soldano** are the three most popular manufacturers in this league. Our example comes from Soldano, and it is the triple-channel **Decatone**, a fine example of what these companies are capable of. This stack has completely independent channels. The clean channel reproduces vintage Fender tones, the crunch is based on vintage Marshall heads, and the lead channel uses circuitry similar to that of the company's own popular **SLO-100** high-gain head. Typically stuffed full of tubes and rather expensive, amps from these companies aim to offer luxury without compromise for the most demanding and discriminating players.

Even more highbrow are the so-called **boutique** amps. Made by smaller, specialist companies from authentic

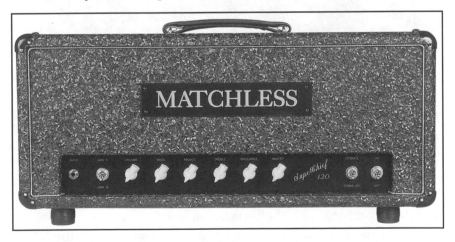

vintage-spec components and using labor-intensive **point-to-point**, hand-wired circuitry, these amps aim to recreate the earliest amp tones. Notable builders include **Dumble** and **Kendrick**, but it is the **Matchless** company that probably enjoys the greatest commercial success. Their **Superchief 120** combo is a 120-watt head with a simple layout in the company's signature retro styling. It focuses on producing a powerful, mellow clean sound with an authentic soft, singing overdrive when pushed hard. Hardly laden with features, it still does what it does flawlessly and appeals to vintage-tone connoisseurs. It is a somewhat acquired and expensive taste.

To segue into the more technical areas of amplification, we have the **Line 6 Flextone** combo. This 1x12 60-watter is one of the new digital-modeling amplifiers that are becoming

Flextone, far right, with AxSys combo and foot controller

increasingly common. In addition to some standard amp controls, the Flextone also features two rotary switches: one for amp model, the other for effects. The digital circuitry can mimic a total of 16 different amp types, including Fender, Marshall, Vox and Soldano best-sellers, then add various combinations of effects, such as echo, chorus, tremolo and reverb. If you don't want a garage full of tube amps and effects pedals—though I personally wouldn't complain—this affordable work of genius could become your flexible friend. Be sure to check out similar amps by Johnson, Tech 21, Art and Yamaha.

Finally, we stray into the techno-mungous land of the rack system. Although the late '80s was the acknowledged heyday of fridge-sized racks, they are still popular among performers with complex tonal requirements. In addition to the basic preamp module and power amp combination, just about anything can be squeezed into these modular cases, including amp heads, studio-style effects units and trays of interconnected stompboxes.

Essentially, a player can assemble all of his or her favorite equipment, be it from the stage, studio, or practice room, and take it on the road in a **flight-case** rack. Although these systems can have any conceivable tone on hand, combining them into a functioning unit can be quite a technical challenge. To achieve this, complex switching systems, often MIDI-based, are built around a **floor controller**—a large board incorporating many foot switches. This enables a player to move from, say, a preset preamp tone with studio chorus to a distortion foot pedal through an amp head, just by tapping one switch.

A world authority on such switching systems is **Bob Bradshaw**, whose services have been used by many famous players, but you will probably need a rock-star salary to pay Bob to sort out your rack.

Some basic rack components:
Preamp

Power Amp

Cab

While you may be drooling over the thought of an omnipotent Bradshaw system, take comfort in the fact that not all racks are unaffordable, nor need they be tremendously complex. In fact, with a few basic units from the many competitively priced lines now available, and a couple of 1x12 speaker cabinets, it is possible to assemble a very powerful rack system for the price of a good combo.

Remember to invest in a tough flight-case module with plenty of extra space (the **SKB** company produces "road-ready" rack modules at very reasonable prices). This will protect your investment and leave room for additional units as you upgrade and expand your system.

Buyer's Guide 5.

If you've paid attention this far, you should be able to stroll into a guitar store, give an amp the once-over and be able to tell what it does, how it does it, and what it probably sounds like when it does. When shopping for an amp your first consideration should be: How much amp do I need? We'll discuss this and subsequent decisions under the heading of application.

Application: Power

Most guitarists are guilty of overkill when it comes to amps, and I speak from personal experience.

As the proud owner of a Marshall stack bought during a dry spell of gigs, I have to admit it impressed visiting friends, but made an expensive and lousy practice amp. When the

gigs eventually came, this 100-watt monster had to be shackled to a modest 3 on the volume setting, so as not to overwhelm the bathroom-sized venues and puny PA

systems. Hardly the hot tube frenzy of distortion I'd spent heaps of cash to enjoy.

The moral of this story: Buy an amp with only as much power as you need. If your amp is intended for playing at home and occasional jamming sessions, then one of the smaller combos of around 12 watts or less should be fine. While designed to sound good at low levels, these little amps can still produce a surprising amount of volume, and they also work well for recording.

If you intend to join a band, then something with a bit more grunt is in order. A medium-powered combo is an ideal candidate, delivering enough output to compete with other instruments, including a drum kit. An output of between 30 and 50 watts is ideal, as the amp will have enough **head-room** (spare power) while still working in the upper ranges of its capabilities, where the best tones live. These medium ratings can be very misleading, as the difference in loudness between 30 and 50 watts is not great, and also because some amps can be louder than others with the same or higher rating. For example, tube amps tend to be modestly rated and can often swamp similarly sized solid-state amps with much higher ratings. Amps with two or more speakers will

seem louder than a combo with only one, as they move more air, but a 1x12 combo will sound more focused and will be more useful in bands with lots of other musicians. The performance of midsized amps varies enormously, but as a rule of thumb aim for 50 watts if the amp is solid-state or hybrid, but try a lower-wattage tube amp first before moving on to more powerful models. This helps avoid overkill with an amp that is barely breaking a sweat instead of working for a living at its full potential.

If you see yourself playing in a loud guitar-based band— probably at a semi-professional level—then one of the larger combos or stack systems could be a wise investment. Before you remortgage your house for a monster Mesa full stack, consider that these big amps were conceived at a time when PA systems were not used to mic guitars, bass and drums,

just the vocals. In those days if you needed a big guitar sound, you needed a huge amp. Today even many small venues have full PA systems, so unless you intend to play larger clubs and concert halls you could well find yourself back in that miserable "on-3" situation to keep the sound engineer happy.

Half stack (right) and stacked combo

If your application does require a stack, then start with a half-stack (a head and single 4x12 cab). This gives you the option to add more speakers should you need to, which is unlikely unless you play Madison Square Garden.

Not recommended for the first-time amp buyer, racks are still a viable option for more experienced players. The beauty of their modular layout means you can start with a simple system and upgrade the components as your playing situation dictates. There is a multitude of rack-compatible gear and infinite setup permutations, so start simple and add on as you go. While magazine reviews and specialist books are certainly good for advice, a serious potential rack user should visit a store with a comprehensive stock of components assembled in a ready-to-play system. This will enable you to try different preamps, effects and power amps together to find the best combination for you. A spare day, friendly staff, and lots of patience and experimenting will get you there in the end.

Player using rack, stack and combo setup

Application: Features

Once you have established how powerful your amp should be, the next consideration is which features it should have. This will largely be determined by the style of music you play, which in turn will determine the basic tone of the amp. Unless you wish to play with a predominantly clean sound, the amount of gain available on the amp will be a major factor. You won't get death metal out of a Roland JC-120. Most players like to use a combination of sounds, both clean and dirty. In this case one of the many dual-channel amps is the best solution. In terms of effects, some folks are happy with a simple splash of reverb; others like to use heaps of effects. If you are a stompbox freak, then an effects loop is going to be mighty handy. Again, overkill is the thing to avoid. If you wish to play with a particular sound then look for an amp that excels at that tone, rather than spending your money on a four channel multi-mode mama, most of which you'll never use. Guitarists have a tendency to get obsessive about tone. By all means buy an amp with a sound you enjoy, but there should be no need to spend thousands on pro-level gear if you are just starting out doing weekend gigs. When you play that wedding function, Aunt Martha will only be disappointed if she can't shake her booty to "Stayin' Alive," not if you don't have a pentode tube rectifier!

Budget

Once you have decided on the size and necessary features of your amp, it's time to look at your savings account. There are so many amps available that there are sure to be a number of models that suit your needs in different price ranges. Once you've decided how much you can afford, collect as much literature as you can, including brochures and magazine reviews, to earmark some likely candidates. However, the best method is to take a trip to a well-stocked music store with your favorite guitar. This will enable you to try lots of different amps to find those that work best with your style and choice of instrument. Keep an open mind and test-drive any amp that fits your needs within your budget—you could be very surprised to find that a cheaper model does everything you desire and still leave you with enough change for a few choice effects. Listen carefully to the tone of the amp and try not to be swayed by ad blurb or "all-tube-snobbery." If it sounds good to you, then it's a good amp for you.

If you have a small budget but still need a powerful amp, there is still hope. Try to track down a simple, high-wattage solid-state combo in the budget price range. The crucial thing here is to find one that can produce a decent and loud clean sound without being too harsh. If it is capable of just this, then you should find that it will work well with a few simple pedals to produce a range of giggable tones. For example, just add a good distortion stompbox and you

essentially have a two-channel amp: clean and distorted. In fact, Joe Satriani's main live sound comes from nothing more than a humble Boss DS-1 distortion pedal played through a clean tube head. Later you could add a chorus pedal to sweeten up the tone, or a delay unit for more texture, but in the meantime you have a workable stage amp.

Used Gear

If your budget is really tight, or you want more for your money, then a used amp can make a lot of sense. Bear in mind that amps can take quite a beating over time, so if an

Scruffy, but working and cheap! A good first-time low-budget contender.

amp looks completely wasted, it probably is just hanging in there and is not a good deal. Try to shop for used gear through a reputable store, where equipment will have had a safety check, and where you can test the amp. The amp may also be covered by a short warranty. If it hasn't had a safety check, ask for one or don't buy it. Old amps can be potentially lethal, so budget a few dollars for a professional once-over if you buy one privately, or if the store hasn't done so, though they certainly should have!

On the subject of buying or selling privately, either through ads or the Internet, please be very careful. Establish beforehand exactly what it is you're buying, the price and any other details. Always send gear and checks by registered courier to minimize risks, and use common sense to protect yourself as much as possible.

Testing, Testing...

If you can, test the amp at high levels. Many stores have a soundproof room for this purpose. The character of amps generally changes as they are pushed harder—normally for the better—but some can show the strain by getting mushy and woolly-sounding. If you already have some favorite effects, then bring them to the showdown as well, to make sure they work with the amp you wish to buy.

Unfortunately, there is no acid test for amps in a live band situation, short of renting a chosen model for a trial. Good ol' common sense and some reliable advice should keep you from landing a turkey, but make sure to check the store's **return policy**—which is normally for exchange within a fixed period of time—just in case the amp doesn't work out. This is especially important if you can't get to a store and need to use **mail order**. Check to see exactly what the return policy covers. Buying any equipment from a store that does not offer one is not recommended.

The Essential Checklist

Once you find yourself with a hot candidate for purchase, keep your wallet firmly in your pocket until you have performed the following checks. If an amp falls down in any of these areas, then there could be trouble ahead.

☐ Speakers

These should sound clear when used with a loud, clean sound. No scratchiness, rattles or other unpleasant noises. If the amp is used, check that the cones have not been ripped or punctured (in closed-back cabs a ripped grille cloth can be a warning sign). If the amp has more than one speaker, listen up close to each at a low volume to make sure they are all working.

☐ Chassis

This should be firmly mounted with no loose switches or sockets, and with the correct complement of fuses. Check for any rust or stains that could mean exposure to dampness or spills. Also be wary of any signs that a used amp has been modified (added controls, altered panel) as this could have been done by an amateur and may be dangerous. If in doubt, *a safety check is a must*.

☐ Controls

These should be wobble-free and smooth to turn. Check for crackles and pops while the amp is running. These could indicate the need for the switches and knobs to be cleaned or possibly even replaced.

☐ Performance

The amp should work well using all channels and switches, at all volumes. If the sound drifts in volume or cuts out there could be serious problems. If there is a loud hum or buzz, even at low volumes, the amp may not be properly grounded. This could be very dangerous. Unplug it and check it, or forget it altogether.

☐ Channels

If the amp has more than one channel, or foot-switchable features, check if a foot switch is available and whether or not it is included with the amp. The foot switch should work reliably and without making any loud clicks through the amp when engaged.

☐ Tubes

If the amp contains tubes, they should be visible from the rear of the cabinet. When the amp is running, have a peek at the chassis to ensure that all the tubes are glowing softly at a similar level. If any are glowing much more brightly than others, or not at all, an expensive tube refit may be necessary. If the amp seems particularly sensitive to vibrations, such as making fluttering or cracking noises when tapped, then this could indicate a tube or connection problem.

☐ Paperwork

New amps should have a warranty from the manufacturer and a return policy from the store. In the case of used amps it is ideal to have a short warranty, and possibly an exchange policy, if bought from a store. Any used amp should have had a safety check. If not, get it to your local amp tech for a service check. Don't risk electrocution or other mishaps for the sake of saving a few dollars!

If you've ticked off all the above and love the tone, then you've just found yourself an amplifier.

Maintenance **6.**

With normal use your amp should need very little maintenance, just some preventative measures and, more importantly, sensible operation. Let's look at several ways to protect both you and your amp.

Safety

Amps plug into the AC supply and you plug your guitar into them. That makes them potentially dangerous. As reit-

Circuit breaker

erated above, your amp should have been safety-tested. If it is more than a few years old, treat it to a full tune up to get the most from your investment. Amps should also be serviced periodically, once a year if you gig regularly.

The single best safety measure you can take is to buy and use a circuit breaker. These are small, inexpensive units that fit between the power outlet and the amp's AC cord. If something goes wrong electrically, then the circuit breaker automatically shuts off the power before it has a chance to get to you. This will protect you and the amp from the dangers of short-circuits and faulty wiring, a real threat in old venues with overloaded electricity supplies. For the cost of a set of strings, these little gizmos cannot be recommended enough, so please make it a habit to use one.

If your amp gets something spilled on it, rained on, dropped, or otherwise injured, unplug it immediately and definitely have it checked out. Although it may still work, a loose connection or electrical short could be lurking within, and it is wise to avoid finding it a lethal way. Similarly, if the amp starts to blow fuses or trips the circuit breaker, something is wrong and it needs looking at, both for safety and to minimize the potential for damage.

Another golden rule of amp safety is to **never use an amp that has the speakers disconnected**. Without a **load** for the power amp to feed, the amp will overheat and cause irreversible damage to the output section. When you go to play always check to be sure any speaker leads are connected *before you switch on*, including those in combos.

Cleaning, Transportation and Storage

With a little care the life of your amp can be greatly increased. Once the amp is safely unplugged, a good spring-cleaning regimen should involve using a vacuum cleaner with a soft attachment to gently remove any accumulated dust from the grille cloth and inside the cabinet Take care not to hit any tubes and keep the nozzle at a safe distance from the chassis. Grubby vinyl covers can be cleaned with a

slightly damp cloth, then immediately rubbed down with a dry cloth. **Never spray water or any cleaning product over your amp!** If a special amp cleaner is used, follow the directions carefully.

If you are using your amp outside of the house, then transport it safely by padding it with blankets and keeping the delicate speakers away from anything pointy like mic stands or case edges. You may wish to invest in a **flight case**. These heavy-duty cases are heavily padded inside and will survive most travel experiences, barring an air crash. Many such cases are lockable and have casters for easier transport. If your amp doesn't have casters, collapsible dollies can be used to move smaller amps, but make sure they are well strapped in. One final transport consideration concerns tube amps. In addition to being rather fragile in any state, tubes are even more fragile when hot. Therefore, avoid moving tube amps immediately after use, especially into extremely cold temperatures. A cooling-down period is essential for prolonged tube life.

Even when your amp is not being used, your thoughts should still be with it. If it didn't come with a soft cover, then consider buying one or covering it with something, like a clean towel. This will keep dust, pet hairs and other amp-unfriendly particles from reaching the parts they shouldn't. Store your amp somewhere dry and safe from extremes of hot and cold. Although the term "woodshedding" refers to practice sessions, the woodshed is not a sensible place to leave your amp.

Tube Replacement

Depending on how frequently and how loud you play, your tubes will need replacing periodically. If the sound begins to grow dull and tired, misbehaves, or just plain dies, then pay a visit to the repairman. The chances are that fresh tubes are needed. This can be a delicate and confusing task, so it is best to have a professional do this for you the first time. But do get them to explain the procedure and write down the tube types so you can do it yourself if you feel confident. The same types of tubes should always be used, unless otherwise advised by the workshop, and must be handled very carefully. **Never change tubes without unplugging your amp from the AC outlet** and don't attempt a tube refit without dependable advice. If you are at all uncertain about the procedure, consult a professional.

Getting Your Tone 7.

Hopefully, all the advice in this book will have landed you a safe and appropriate amp, and helped you understand what goes on inside our Tolex-covered friends. Chances are you will have chosen an amp for the range of tones it can produce, but you may not be sure how to get the best from them. The following are some pointers to set up your amp for optimum use, but remember, this is just a guide. There is no "correct" way to set an amp, so make sure you take some time for experimental knob-twiddling.

Setting Your Sounds

As mentioned earlier, the best place to start with an amp is with the tone controls set flat. If your amp has a single channel, dial in as much gain as you wish, then adjust the tone controls to find your chosen sound. Increasing the bass will add fatness and rumble, increasing the treble will add brightness and bite, and changing the mid control(s) will have the most dramatic effect of all. With the mid control turned down the tone with be hollow, or scooped, and up high will add both punch and thickness. By balancing these

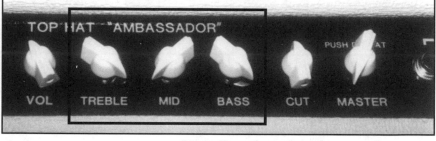

"Scooped" sound

controls, quite different tones can be produced. Listen to the tone when flat, then try setting the bass and treble high and the mid at zero. With low gain you will have a hollow, stinging clean sound (used in funk and reggae); with high gain it will sound chunky and aggressive—perfect for metal riffing.

Now try the opposite settings with the mid up high and the bass and treble low. This "humped" setting produces a round,

"Humped" sound

warm, clean sound and a similarly thick distortion. Both make good lead tones. These opposite settings represent some of the more exaggerated tones of your amp, but most players find their favored sounds to be somewhere in between.

With gain and reverb controls there is a big temptation to overshoot, especially for live playing, which results in a muddy, confused tone. Try backing these off at higher volumes and you will be rewarded with more detail and clarity, but hey, sometimes swamped-out super-gain can be a lot of fun!

Multi-Channels

If your amp has more than one channel, then the key is to set the separate volumes at realistic levels. You may want one channel to be louder than another, but if it is hugely louder then it just won't work in a band situation. You may want to sound like Armageddon when it comes to your solo, but if you can't hear the rest of the band you'll just sound dumb. Different channel volumes can really help dynamics, but check that ego in at the front desk.

Using Effects

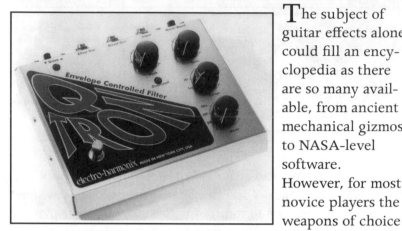

The subject of guitar effects alone could fill an encyclopedia as there are so many available, from ancient mechanical gizmos to NASA-level software.

However, for most novice players the weapons of choice are usually stompboxes or a **floor-mounted multi-effects processor**. Let's deal with the multi-processor choice first.

These processors range from a simple unit that combines a few effects to more complex programmable units with just about everything on board. Either way, it is best to start with a balanced, clean sound on the amp, then try the unit plugged directly into the amp—and also through the effects loop if it has one—and go with the choice that sounds best. The more complex processors are weird to use because they are intended to take the raw guitar sound and shape it to completion, without much room for the amp's own capabilities. If you prefer the sound of your amp's distortion you

need to edit your processor patches to remove the distortion in high-gain settings. Similar judicious reprogramming will enable the amp's clean tones to be used without

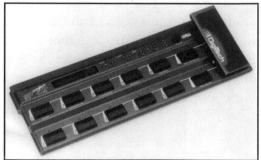

sounding over-processed. The bottom line with multi-effects is to do some serious tweaking and comparisons until you get the best from both your amp and effects.

Single-effects pedals are far more straightforward because they just do what it says on the box. There is certainly no legislation when it comes to stompboxes; try them in different sequences and at different levels and you will probably come up with some original tones of your own. As a starting point, the
accepted chain of command from guitar to amp is: compressor, wah, distortion, chorus, delay, then any other digital effects. If your amp has an effects loop, use it to separate the time-based effects: chorus, delay, flanger, etc. This sequence should produce a quiet and efficient effects chain, but it is wise to do some juggling of your own. As with amps, set the effects flat to begin with, then balance the various controls to taste. The only units that you need to be a little careful with are octavers and those that produce a large boost in volume; there is a small chance that they may damage the amp at extreme settings, so be sure to start with a low level

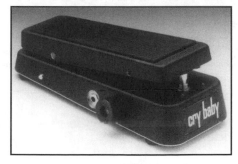 on these guys and gradually work up.

Happy amping! I hope this book will help you find that special amp and enjoy your gain without pain. Have fun and play safe.

Additional Guides from Hal Leonard Corporation

Ampeg: The Story Behind the Sound
by Gregg Hopkins and Bill Moore

Ampeg: The Story Behind the Sound tells the tale of this extraordinary company on its 50th anniversary, weaving together the American success story of the company founder, the role of key investors and inventions, and the development of innovative music equipment products—all against the background of American pop music and corporate competition in the music industry. Many Ampeg endorsees are profiled, including Johnny Smith, James Jamerson, Donald "Duck" Dunn, Gary Karr, Victor Wooten, Bill Wyman, Jason Newsted, Michael Anthony, and more. The result provides something of interest to musicians, collectors, and those who lived part of the history. Includes more than 200 photos and a 32-page color section.

00330289 ....(288 pages, 8-1/2" X 11") $32.95

Amps! The Other Half of Rock 'n' Roll
by Ritchie Fliegler

This book provides the first overall view of amps, including: how amps work, profiles of the major manufacturers, "transistor dinosaurs" and their place in amp history, reissues vs. vintage amps, and troubleshooting. Terms are defined in the margin as they are introduced, and plenty of photos and diagrams illuminate the text.

00330057...(128 pages, 9" X 12") $24.95

The Art of the Amplifier
by Michael Doyle

The Art of the Amplifier pays tribute to the mechanical and aesthetic beauty of the tube amp, focusing on guitar amplifiers but also examining hi-fi audio amps and very ornate early radios. The book contains 80 stunning full-color pages, nearly 200 photos and informative commentary, with amplifiers grouped by manufacturers. Represented are Ampeg, Dumble, Fender, Groove Tubes, Gibson, Gretsch, Hi Fi, Marshall, Mesa Boogie, Peavey, Vox, Watkins and many others.

00330002...(80 pages, 9" X 12") $22.95

A Desktop Reference of Hip Vintage Guitar Amps
by Gerald Weber

If you have questions about guitar amplifiers–how to fix them, restore them, or hot-rod them—this book has the answer. This book is written for the guitarist or collector who desires a commonsense approach to understanding the essence of vintage tube amps and vintage tube tone. Not written for engineers, it does not contain engineering formulas, polar mathematic equations, or abbreviations that you are assumed to know. Gerald Weber, a regular columnist for Vintage Guitar magazine, shares the knowledge he has accumulated over the years of repairing and building his line of Kendrick amps.

00330225...(507 pages, 6" X 9") $26.95

The Fender Amp Book
A Complete History of Fender Amplifiers
By John Morrish

A full-color journey through the entire development of the famous Fender amplifier – from the "tweed" amps of the 1950s and '60s to current designs. This book features 120 color photos of classic and modern Fender amps and a detailed reference section for collectors. Incorporating material drawn from interviews with key Fender personnel, The Fender Amp Book tells the absorbing story of one of the most important product lines of one of the most successful electric instrument companies.

00330148...(96 pages, 4-3/4" X 9-1/4") $17.95

Fender Amps–The First Fifty Years
by Teagle and Sprung

Includes detailed model features and specs, rare catalog reprints, classic advertisements, endorsee promo photos, and hundreds of close-up photos of these American beauties. Includes a 40-page full-color section (complete with a two-page pullout group shot of over 60 amps!), and the choicest vintage catalog covers. Also includes sections on how amps work, basic amp maintenance, setup tips, and detailed parts info necessary for dating and restoring Fender amps.
00697278 ....(256 pages, 8-1/2" X 11") $34.95

A History of Marshall Valve Guitar Amplifiers 1962-1992
by Michael Doyle

Doyle combines detailed chronologies of the various model and serial numbers, straightforward explanations of their features and construction, and aesthetic evaluations of the results. The book is dotted with the names of rock luminaries and peppered with photos—well over 100 black-and-white ones, plus a 32-page color section and a 32-page full-color appendix that reproduces all of the Marshall catalogs of the '60s.
00330058...(256 pages, 9" X 12") $32.95

Tube Amp Talk for the Guitarist and Tech
by Gerald Weber

For this follow-up to his popular *A Desktop Reference of Hip Vintage Guitar Amps*, Gerald Weber has compiled his articles and "Ask Gerald" columns that have appeared in Vintage Guitar magazine from 1993 to 1996. As a special bonus, Ken Fisher's "Trainwreck Pages" from Vintage Guitar are also included. This book assumes that the reader has at least a working knowledge of tube guitar amplifiers, and it will be helpful and interesting whether or not guitarists intend to perform their own servicing.
00330380 ....(537 pages 6" X 9") $29.95

Tube Amp Basics for the Guitarist
by Gerald Weber

In this video you'll learn the "plain talk" basics that every guitar player should know. You'll learn commonsense troubleshooting techniques that can be done without any special equipment. You'll learn the basic layout of the guitar amp and how to isolate problems so they can be solved. You'll learn correct procedure if a fuse blows, or if you plug in and there's no sound. You'll even learn the contents of the "first aid kit" that should go to every gig. It's an hour of essential tube amp knowledge. 60 minutes.
00320145 ....VHS Video $29.95

FOR MORE INFORMATION, SEE YOUR LOCAL MUSIC DEALER,
OR WRITE TO:

HAL•LEONARD®
CORPORATION
7777 W. BLUEMOUND RD. P.O. BOX 13819 MILWAUKEE, WI 53213

Visit our website at
www.halleonard.com

Guitar World Presents: The Bonehead's Guides

The Bonehead's Guide to Guitars

by Dominic Hilton

Don't know your tremolo from your truss rod? Fear not, this book will guide you through the essential differences between various electric guitars with clear explanations of how they work, how they sound and how their parts function. Learn about the effect that different construction, woods and components have on the tone of a guitar, and how to use this knowledge to get the most from your instrument or track down your ideal electric.

This guide also includes vital information on which guitar to choose for your style of playing and budget, and how to avoid buying a problem instrument. It also contains valuable advice on maintaining and upgrading your guitar, and covers all of the safety precautions associated with using an electrified instrument.
00695332 .... $9.95

The Bonehead's Guide to Amps

by Dominic Hilton

For many novice players the amp is the boring, functional part of their first setup. This guide explains how it can be as exciting, inspirational and important as their guitar. Viewing the amp as an instrument in its own right, this book defines both the fundamental and subtle differences between many types of amplifiers, while offering valuable info on "tone-tweaking" every kind to suit different styles. Learn how to adjust your amp for a whole range of different tones and how to use its functions to maximum effect.

By taking an objective and comprehensive view of available guitar amps, this book offers the best bang-for-buck advice on getting killer tones easily, affordably, and blasting at the right level. If you want to get your guitar cooking, then make sure it has the right ingredients with this invaluable guide.
00695334 .... $9.95

The Bonehead's Guide to Effects

by Dominic Hilton

The bizarre technology of guitar effects uses everything from feet to floppy disks, and this guide provides the necessary knowledge to choose and use these weird devices according to your style and budget. If you feel the urge to wah, flange, uni-vibe or pitch-shift, then this is the book to get you effected.

The Bonehead's Guide to Effects gets right to the point with an illustrated description of every type of guitar effect, including its sound, application and the various formats available. From a simple "stompbox" to high-powered rack systems, all are clearly explained in terms of how they function and how they can be used to enhance your playing.

The text includes a detailed buyer's guide to assembling your ideal effects system, alongside useful safety and maintenance tips. There is also vital info on "chaining" effects and recipes for basic tones and outrageous sounds.
00695333 .... $9.95

FOR MORE INFORMATION, SEE YOUR LOCAL MUSIC DEALER,
OR WRITE TO:

HAL•LEONARD®
CORPORATION

7777 W. BLUEMOUND RD. P.O. BOX 13819 MILWAUKEE, WI 53213

Visit our website at
www.halleonard.com